THE CAT'S ELBOW

and Other Secret Languages

Omtay's auntway asway icksay.*
Eshay askedway imhay otay ogay otay erhay officeway andway etgay erhay aycheckpay orfay erhay. Utbay onway ethay ayway omehay, Omtay asway obbedray!

Enwhay ehay awsay away oliceman-pay, ehay outedshay, "Somebody stole my aunt's pay! Somebody stole my aunt's pay!"

"Allway ightray, idkay," ethay olice-manpay aidsay. "Utcay outway ethay Igpay Atinlay andway elltay emay atwhay appenedhay."

* To translate this, see page 5.

THE CAT'S ELBOW

AND OTHER
SECRET LANGUAGES

Collected by *Alvin Schwartz*
Pictures by *Margot Zemach*

FARRAR STRAUS GIROUX
New York

First printing, 1982
Printed in the United States of America
Published simultaneously in Canada by
McGraw-Hill Ryerson Ltd., Toronto

Designed by Charlotte Staub

"The Old Woman and the Pig" on page 56 is
reprinted and adapted from "The Boonville Language
of Northern California" by Lynwood Carranco
and Wilma R. Simmons, *American Speech*, v. 39, no. 4,
by permission of the University of Alabama Press;
Copyright © 1964 by the University of Alabama Press

Library of Congress Cataloging in Publication Data
The Cat's elbow and other secret languages.
    Bibliography: p.   Summary: Presents instructions
for speaking thirteen secret languages including
Pig Latin, one of the best known and easiest codes
to learn, and Boontling, developed by people
in a California town.
    1. Ciphers—Juvenile literature.   2. Cryptography—
Juvenile literature.   [1. Ciphers.   2. Cryptography]
I. Schwartz, Alvin.   II. Zemach, Margot.
Z103.3.C38   652′.8   81–5513
ISBN 0-374-31224-9   AACR2

Foforor
Anondodrorewow,
onone cocoolol cocatot

CONTENTS

THE
CAT'S
ELBOW
and Other Secret Languages

Gogeroraloldod Kokisossosedod Mome!

To keep a secret like the one above, use a secret language. It will keep outsiders from eavesdropping.[1]

It also will make you feel mysterious. Some words may sound silly to other people, but *only* you and your friends will know that "ketchiggityupiggity" means "ketchup" and that "dot hog" means "hot dog."

Children all over the world speak in secret languages, but they are not the only ones. Spies, smugglers, and thieves also do. So do members of secret societies. So do peddlers and shopkeepers. So do lovers. So do parents when they don't want children to know what is being said. In fact, some parents use a secret language they knew when they were young.

Most secret languages aren't complicated—if you know the secret. By adding a special letter to each word, or by moving a syllable or making some other change, you can turn any language into a secret language.

There are hundreds of these languages. There even is one which involves whistling. And there is another one in which people talk by beating on drums. In the notes at the back, there is more information on these.

Many years ago, a town in California had its own secret language. The language was called Boontling. Everybody who lived in that town spoke it. But nobody else could figure it out.

Speaking a secret language isn't hard. All it takes is practice. Just find a friend who wants to learn. Then every day talk to one another in your secret language.

Start by translating a word or phrase in each sentence: "Let's go to the oozay!"[2] "She's a creepbeep!"[3] "You're a dodolollol!"[4] Then try short sentences. Then try longer ones.

In the beginning, you will speak very slowly. You also will not understand everything your partner says. But in a few weeks it will be as easy as iepay.[5] And nobody will understand what you are saying except your fofrorienondod.[6]

1 *To translate the secret, see page 37.*

2 *See page 5.*

3 *See page 25.*

4 *See page 37.*

5 *See page 5.*

6 *See page 37.*

I. PIG LATIN

This is one of the best-known secret languages. It also is one of the easiest to learn. People used to say that even a pig could learn it. Which is why it is called Pig Latin.

To speak Pig Latin

1. Move the first letter in a word to the end of the word. Then add "ay."

hamburger   amburger-hay

2. If a word starts with two consonants or more, move these letters to the end of the word. Then add "ay."

<u>ch</u>eese   eese-<u>chay</u>

3. If a word starts with a vowel, don't move the vowel. Instead, add "way" to the word.

<u>o</u>nion   onion-<u>way</u>

Practice Riddles

What is the best way to catch a rabbit?
Ide-hay ehind-bay a-way ush-bay and-way ake-may a-way oise-nay ike-lay a-way arrot-cay.

What has fur like a coyote, howls like a coyote, and is made of cement?
A-way oyote-cay. I-way ut-pay in-way e-thay ement-cay o-tay ake-may it-way arder-hay.

Why did the traffic light turn red?

Ou-yay ould-way urn-tay ed-ray, oo-tay, if-way ou-yay ad-hay o-tay ange-chay in-way ont-fray of-way all-way ose-thay eople-pay.

What do you call a friendly, helpful monster?
A-way ailure-fay.

For the solutions to the practice problems, turn to page 63.

E-thay ext-nay anguage-lay is-way "Iggity-way."

2. IGGITY

At one time, many languages were called Pig Latin, not just the language in the first chapter. There also were others called Hog Latin and Dog Latin. And most of these worked in the same way.

After each syllable, a special sound was added. In Albany, New York, this sound was "iggity." In other places, it was "gree," "guy," "ire," "ly," "ki," or "snikes," or some other sound.

"Iggity" is used in the examples below, but any of these sounds could be used in the same way.

To speak Iggity

After each syllable, add the sound "iggity."

Hot   Hot-iggity
chili   chil-iggity-i-iggity
and   and-iggity
crackers crack-iggity-ers-iggity.

Practice Rhymes

There was an old man from Peru
Who dreamed he was eating his shoe.
    He awoke in the night
    With a terrible fright
And-iggity found-iggity he-iggity was-iggity eat-iggity-ing-
    iggity his-iggity shoe-iggity.

There was a young woman from Lynn
Who was unusually thin.
    One day in the shade
    She sipped lemonade
And-iggity slipped-iggity through-iggity the-iggity straw-
    iggity and-iggity fell-iggity in-iggity.

There was an old lady from Kent
Whose nose was terribly bent.
    But she chose
    To follow her nose
And-iggity no-iggity-bod-iggity-y-iggity knows-iggity where-
    iggity she-iggity went-iggity.

The-iggity next-iggity lan-iggity-guage-iggity is-iggity "Ku-iggity."

3. KU

This language was spoken by children in Chernovsty, a city in the southwestern corner of Russia. It works in just the opposite way that Iggity does. With Iggity, you add a special sound after each syllable. With Ku, you add such a sound *before* each syllable.

To speak Ku

Start each syllable with "ku."

You	Ku-you
are	ku-are
a	ku-a
donkey!	ku-don-ku-key!

Practice

Famous sayings:

"Don't touch me, or I'll scream!" ku-the ku-si-ku-ren ku-said ku-to ku-the ku-po-ku-lice-ku-man.

"I'm getting that rundown feeling," ku-the ku-cow ku-said ku-as ku-she ku-wan-ku-der-ku-ed ku-down ku-the ku-road.

"This is really easy," ku-the ku-girl ku-said, ku-fall-ku-ing ku-off ku-a ku-log.

"Pretty swell joint you have here," ku-the ku-doc-ku-tor ku-said ku-as ku-he ku-look-ku-ed ku-at ku-the ku-pa-ku-tient's ku-knee.

Ku-the ku-next ku-lan-ku-guages ku-are "Ku-ob-ku-by-Ku-dob-ku-by," "Ku-egg-ku-o-Ku-peg-ku-go," ku-and "Ku-ip."

4. OBBY-DOBBY, EGGO-PEGGO, IP

Obby-Dobby and Eggo-Peggo are used in most English-speaking countries. Ip is spoken on the island of Jamaica in the Caribbean Sea. To speak these languages, add the special sounds described below.

To speak Obby-Dobby

Insert the sound "ob" before each vowel.

I	Ob-i
love	l-ob-ov-ob-e
you!	y-ob-o-ob-u!

To speak Eggo-Peggo

Insert the sound "egg" before each vowel.

Let's	L-egg-et's
get	g-egg-et
married!	m-egg-arr-egg-i-egg-ed!

To speak Ip

Insert the sound "ip" before each vowel.

Okay!   Ip-ok-ip-ay!

Practice Riddles

What did George Washington's father say when he saw George's report card?

"G-ob-e-ob-org-ob-e, y-ob-o-ob-u ob-ar-ob-e g-ob-o-ob-ing d-ob-ow-n ob-in h-ob-ist-ob-ory."

Why does a stork stand on one leg?

Ob-if ob-it d-ob-idn't, ob-it w-ob-o-ob-uld f-ob-all d-ob-own.

What do cheerleaders drink before every game?
R-egg-o-egg-ot b-egg-e-egg-er.

How do you keep a skunk from smelling?
Y-ip-o-ip-u h-ip-old ip-its n-ip-os-ip-e.

Th-ip-e n-ip-ext l-ip-ang-ip-u-ip-ag-ip-e ip-is "K-ip-iny-ip-um-ip-e."

5. KINYUME

Some children talk backwards when they have a secret to keep. To say a word, they start with the last letter. Then they work their way toward the beginning of the word. In this way, "secret" becomes "t-e-r-c-e-s," and "language" becomes "e-g-a-u-g-n-a-l." But this can get complicated.

Children in East Africa had an easier way of talking backwards. When they said a word, they reversed the order of the syllables. That way, the last syllable was first and the first syllable was last. They called their backwards language Kinyume.

To speak Kinyume

1. If a word has two syllables, move the last syllable to the beginning of the word.

tiger   ger-ti
lion   on-li
cobra   ra-cob

2. If a word has more than two syllables, move the last syllable to the beginning of the word. Move the first syllable to the end of the word.

crocodile   dile-o-croc
elephant   phant-e-el
gorilla   la-ril-go

3. If a word has only one syllable, move the last letter or sound to the beginning of the word. Move the first letter or sound to the end of the word.

run   n-u-r
chase   se-a-ch
shoot   t-oo-sh

Practice

Tom S. Cat speaks Kinyume:

"I wove this basket," id-sa M-o-t S. ly-i-craft.

"I sing in the choir," id-sa M-o-t S. ly-ful-glee.
"E-b ful-care th-wi at-th e-knif," said Tom S. cuttingly.
"T-ha-w o-d en-sev s-ay-d ke-ma?" asked Tom S. weakly.

E-h-t t-ex-n guage-lan s-i "B Guage-lan."

6. B LANGUAGE

This is a German secret language. You repeat each syllable in every word, and the words get longer and sillier. Each of these new syllables starts with the letter "B." That is why this language is called B Language. It is what the girls in the picture are saying—in sign language.

To speak B Language

1. Repeat each syllable.
2. If a new syllable starts with a consonant, replace the consonant with the letter "B."

nuts	nuts-<u>b</u>uts
raisins	rai-<u>b</u>ai-sins-<u>b</u>ins
fudge	fudge-<u>b</u>udge

3. If a new syllable starts with a vowel, keep the vowel and add "B."

orange	or-<u>b</u>or-ange-<u>b</u>ange
ice cream	ice-<u>b</u>ice cream-<u>b</u>eam

4. If a new syllable starts with double letters (like "bl" in "blood"), replace the double letters with just the letter "b."

blood	<u>bl</u>ood-<u>b</u>ood
ghost	<u>gh</u>ost-<u>b</u>ost

5. The new syllable should rhyme with the old syllable. If it doesn't, change the sounds slightly so that it does rhyme when you pronounce it.

"Blood-bood" should sound like "blood-bud."

"Ghost-bost" should sound like "ghost-boast."

Practice Jokes

Teacher: Sam, your spelling is getting much better. You only made five mistakes.

Sam: Thank you.

Teacher: Now-bow, let's-bet's look-book at-bat the-be next-bext word-bord.

"Did you hear about the fight in the bakery?"

"No."

"A-ba dough-bough-nut-but got-bot fresh-besh."

"Did you hear about the boy who knocked on the lamp-post?"

"No."

"The-be light-bite was-bas on-bon. So-bo he-be thought-bought that-bat some-bome-bod-bod-y-by was-bas home-bome up-bup-stairs-bairs."

"Did you hear about the girl who took the school bus home?"

"No."

"Her-ber moth-both-er-ber made-bade her-ber take-bake it-bit back-back."

The-be next-bext lan-ban-guage-buage is-bis "Sa-Ba-La-Ba."

7. SA-LA

Children in the city of Amoy, in China, spoke Sa-La over a hundred years ago. In this language, each syllable becomes *three* syllables. If you speak Sa-La rapidly, some of the words will sound like tiny bells tinkling.

To speak Sa-La

1. Repeat each syllable twice. The first time, start the new syllable with the letter "l." The second time, start the new syllable with the letter "s."

king   king-ling-sing
queen   queen-leen-seen
throne throne-lone-sone

2. The two new syllables should rhyme with the old syllable. If they don't, change their sounds slightly so that they do rhyme when you pronounce them.

"The-le-se" should sound like "the-luh-suh."

Practice Rhymes

A peanut
sat
on the railroad track,
its heart all a-flutter.
A-la-sa-long-long-song came-lame-same
the-le-se morn-lorn-sorn-ing-ling-sing train-lain-sain—
pea-lea-sea-nut-lut-sut but-lut-sut-ter-ler-ser!

A frog
sat
on the end
of a log
watch-latch-satch-ing-ling-sing a-la-sa tad-lad-sad-pole-lole-
    sole
turn-lurn-surn in-lin-sin-to-lo-so—
a-la-sa frog-log-sog.

The-le-se next-lext-sext lan-lan-san-guage-luage-suage is-lis-sis "Med-led-sed-i-li-si-cal-lal-sal Greek-leek-seek."

8. MEDICAL GREEK

When medical students in England felt like fooling around, they spoke a secret language called Medical Greek. They did not translate every word into this language—only those words they thought would sound silly. Of course, Medical Greek has nothing to do with Greek, just as Pig Latin has nothing to do with Latin.

To speak Medical Greek

1. In each sentence, try to find two words that are connected in some way. These would be words like "bread and

butter," "climb a tree," "fat pig," and "lamb chop." Exchange the first letters or sounds in these words.

bread and butter   bed and brutter
climb a tree   trimb a clee
lamb chop   chamb lop
fat pig   pat fig

2. In each sentence, also look for a long word. Pick out two syllables in this word. Exchange the first letters or sounds.

hamburger   bam-hurg-er
touchdown   dutch-town
downtown   town-down

Practice

The Story of the Bicious Vull

Two men dudsenly chere warged by a bicious vull. One of them trimbed a clee. The other jumped into a heep dole, but he jept kumping out. When the chull barged at him, he bumped jack in. Then dudsenly he bumped jack out, tran for the ree and climbed it.

"Why aren't you in hat thole?" his friend asked.

"Well," he said, "bar's a th'ar in hat thole."

The lext nanguage is "The Elt's Cabow."

9. THE CAT'S ELBOW

In this language, extra letters are added to each word. The Cat's Elbow is a German secret language. Why does it have such a curious name? It was the name the Germans gave to the funny bone and perhaps to other things they thought were slightly crazy. Of course, cats *do* have elbows. They are the joints in their front legs.

To speak The Cat's Elbow

After each consonant, add the vowel "o," then repeat the consonant. Each vowel remains as it is.

cat   c<u>oc</u>-a-t<u>ot</u>
mouse   m<u>om</u>-ou-s<u>os</u>-e
purr   p<u>op</u>-u-r<u>or</u>-ror
squeak   s<u>os</u>-q<u>oq</u>-uea-k<u>ok</u>
pounce   p<u>op</u>-ou-n<u>on</u>-c<u>oc</u>-e

Practice

Hard questions:

There was
a goose between two geese,
a goose behind two geese,
a goose ahead of two geese.
How many geese were there?

Tot-hoh-ror-e-e.

How can a cat have three tails?

No cat has two tails.
One cat has one tail more than no cat.
Tot-hoh-e-ror-e-fof-o-ror-e, o-non-e coc-a-tot hoh-a-sos tot-
hoh-ror-e-e tot-a-i-lol-sos.

Two fathers and two sons went fishing. They each caught a fish. But together they only caught three fish. How could this be?

Tot-hoh-e pop-e-o-pop-lol-e wow-hoh-o wow-e-non-tot fof-i-sos-hoh-i-non-gog wow-e-ror-e a bob-o-yoy, hoh-i-sos fof-a-tot-hoh-e-ror, a-non-dod hoh-i-sos gog-ror-a-non-dod-fof-a-tot-hoh-e-ror. Tot-hoh-e bob-o-yoy'-sos gog-ror-a-non-dod-fof-a-tot-hoh-e-ror a-lol-sos-o wow-a-sos hoh-i-sos fof-a-tot-hoh-e-ror'-sos fof-a-tot-hoh-e-ror.

Tot-hoh-e non-e-xox-tot lol-a-non-gog-u-a-gog-e i-sos "Zoz-i-pop-hoh."

10. ZIPH

If you learn to speak Ziph properly, people may think you are talking in tongue twisters. A famous writer named Thomas De Quincey used Ziph as a secret language when he was a boy. He learned it from his doctor one time when he was sick. That was in England in the 1790s.

To speak Ziph

After each vowel, add the letter "g," then repeat the vowel. Each consonant remains as it is:

elephant	e̲ge-l-e̲ge-ph-a̲ga-nt
flea	fl-ege-aga
hippopotamus	higip-po̲go-pogot-aga-mugus

Practice

An endless tale:

I laughed so hard, I thought I'd die.
I did die.
Th-ege-y b-ugu-r-igi-ege-d m-ege,
Aga-nd aga l-igi-ttl-ege fl-ogo-w-ege-r
   gr-ege-w ogo-n my gr-aga-v-ege.
B-ugu-t th-ege r-ogo-ogo-ts gr-ege-w d-ogo-wn aga-nd t-igi-
    ckl-ege-d m-ege . . .
(*Start over with the first line.*)

Th-ege n-ege-xt l-aga-ng-ugu-aga-g-ege igi-s "K-igi-ng T-ugu-t."

11. KING TUT

This is a secret spelling language which is used in the United States. It also is called Double Dutch and Tutney. There are many such languages in both Europe and America.

Each spelling language uses a special alphabet in which the letters have new sounds. These are sounds like "bub" for "b" and "cut" for "c." When you speak in a spelling language, replace the old sounds with the new ones.

To speak King Tut

1. Learn the sounds of the letters in the alphabet on the next page. The sounds for "Q" and "X" remain the same. So do the sounds for the vowels.

A - a   I - i   R - rur
B - bub   J - jug   S - sus
C - cut   K - kam   T - tut
D - dud   L - lul   U - u
E - e   M - mum   V - vuv
F - fuf   N - nun   W - wuv
G - gug   O - o   Y - yec
H - hush   P - pup   Z - zuz

2. In speaking King Tut, spell out each word you use, replacing the usual sounds with the new ones above.

mummy   mum-u-mum-mum-yec
tomb   tut-o-mum-bub
pyramid   pup-yec-rur-a-mum-i-dud
camel   cut-a-mum-e-lul

Practice

Did you ever see
a catfish?

a catwalk?

a bub-a-rur-nun dud-a-nun-cut-e?

a-nun o-cut-e-a-nun wuv-a-vuv-e?

a mum-o-o-nun-bub-e-a-mum?

a pup-e-a-nun-u-tut sus-tut-a-nun-dud?

a bub-a-rur-bub-e-rur sus-hush-o-pup?

a kam-i-tut-cut-hush-e-nun sus-i-nun-kam?

Tut-hush-e nun-e-x-tut lul-a-nun-gug-u-a-gug-e i-sus "Tut-hush-i-e-fuf Tut-a-lul-kam."

12. THIEF TALK

Thieves and other criminals have used a secret language for as long as they have practiced their trade. In fact, some words they use today were in use over five hundred years ago. These include "to cop," or to steal; "cush," or money; and "stir," or prison.

This language helps thieves to conceal their plans. It also helps to bring thieves together. In the nineteenth century it was known in some places as "flash," or as "Peddler's French." But today it does not have a name.

Thief Talk actually is a code in which certain words stand for other words. "Oliver" means moon, "Tommy" means bread, "bam" is a lie, and "forks" are fingers.

It also has words which rhyme with the words they stand for. "Twist and twirl" is a girl. "Tea-leaf" is a thief. "Apple pies" are eyes. This rhyming slang first was used in the rough Cockney section of London. But the rhymes are not used as often as they once were. Now, just "twist" may be a girl, and just "apple" may be an eye.

To speak Thief Talk

Use everyday language, but replace any words you want to keep secret with words from Thief Talk. See the list below. Add to it with secret words and rhymes of your own.

Practice

A Poem in Thief Talk

As I sat in front of the Anna Maria
Warming me plates of meat
There came a knock at the Rory O'More
That made me old raspberry beat.

Words from Thief Talk

bank - Frank and Hank
beef stew - garlic and glue
boy - pride and joy
bread - Tommy
child - greasy chin
chin - Andy McGuinn
coat - tog

dance - kick and prance
dinner - Johnny Skinner
dirty - quisby
dishonest - cross
doctor - bolus
dog, watch-dog - buffer
dollar - hoot and holler

door - Rory O'More
to eat - to souse
executioner - Johnny Grab
eyes - apple pies, meat pies
face - Chevy Chase
feet - plates of meat
fingers - forks
fire - Anna Maria
to follow - to fox
gambler - carder
girl - twist and twirl
heart - raspberry tart
hog - antelope
jail - moan and wail
judge - wig
knees - bugs and fleas
knife - chiv
legs - bacon and eggs
a lie - bam
a big lie - hummer
money - blunt
moon - Oliver
murderer - croaksman
name - chant
"Give me your name" -
   "Tip your chant"

nickel - half a hog
no - Brown Joe
to pick pockets - to knuck
pickpocket - knucker
pistol - pop
rifle (gun) - sharp
river - moat
road - frog and toad
shirt - skin
shoes and boots - crabs
sick - half a tick
sleep - Little Bo Peep
stairs - apples and pears
steak - Joe Blake
stomach - crammer
store - chorey
to talk - to mang
thief - outer
toes - these and those
a walk - a ball of chalk
a watch - a thimble
"What time is it?" -
   "What circle?"
to write - to scroll
worthless person - dot
yes - Brown Bess

Now, greasy chin, let's mang Boontling!

13. BOONTLING

"Boontling" stands for Boonville lingo, a secret language that a whole town once used. The town was Boonville, California, an isolated place a hundred miles north of San Francisco. From the 1880s to the 1930s, almost everybody in and around Boonville spoke Boontling as naturally as they spoke English.

A young woman was an "applehead." A young man was a "kimmey" or a "tweed." When they went to a dance, they "piked to a hob." If it was a good dance, it was a "bal hob." If it was no good, it was "nonch." Afterwards they might have supper and talk; that is, have "chiggrel and harp." Then they would go home—they would "pike to their region."

Some say that children started this language so that they could keep secrets from their parents. Others say grownups started it to keep secrets from their children. Whatever the case, in a few years everybody in and around Boonville was "harpin' Boont." There were over a thousand words they used in combination with English.

But outsiders could not make heads or tails of them. As far as they were concerned, it was a secret language. It was one of the things that made Boontling fun to use. Sometimes an outsider pretended to understand, but usually he didn't fool anybody.

Boontling also had practical uses. When the town baseball players had a game, they never used signals. They called to one another in Boont. When men from Boonville went to war, they wrote home in Boont, and their letters were never censored.

There were two things that made Boontling hard for outsiders to understand. There were no rules they could learn. And there were few words that were like those in other languages.

Eventually, many people who used the language moved away or died. As Boonville changed and grew, and lost its isolation, Boontling began to slowly die out. Some people still "harp the lingo" now and then, but more and more know nothing about it.

To speak Boontling

Use the language in combination with English. A list of words is on pages 58–60. If you need more words, make them up in ways that Boonters did.

Base a word on how somebody looks or behaves or spends his or her time.

"Bearman" is the word in Boontling for "storyteller." It comes from the fact that the best storyteller in town was a man who hunted bears. "Jeffer" is the word for "fire." It also is the name of a man who liked to make big fires. "High pockety" means "rich." Where did that come from? The richest man in town also was the tallest man and had the highest pockets.

Base a word on how something sounds.

"Spat" is the word in Boontling for a .22 caliber bullet. It is also something like the sound you hear when the bullet is fired. "To charl" means "to milk a cow." When milk from a cow hits the inside of a bucket, it makes a sound something like "charl."

Make one word from two words.

"Schoolch" is Boontling for "schoolteacher." It includes "school" and part of "teacher." "Relf" is a rail fence. "Toobs" is the word for twenty-five cents, or two bits, or "two" + "b."

Practice

This is the ancient tale of "The Old Woman and the Pig" as it was told many years ago in Boonville.

The Eeld'm and the Borp

An eeld'm found some forbes and buckeys and felt high-pockety. So she piked to Boont and used her higs for a borp.

On her way region, the eeld'm had to pike over a relf. But borp wouldn't pike, and she couldn't jape him region, and she wanted her chiggrel.

Soon a hareem piked by, and the eeld'm harped, "Hareem, hareem, chiggrel borp, borp won't jump relf and pike region, and I'll get no chiggrel." But hareem noned.

Eeld'm got cocked and harped to a stick, "Stick, stick, dreek hareem, hareem won't chiggrel borp, borp won't jump relf and pike region, and I'll get no chiggrel." But stick noned.

Soon she met a jeffer. Still in a greeny, she harped, "Jeffer, jeffer, ark stick, stick won't dreek hareem, hareem won't chiggrel borp, borp won't jump relf and pike region, and I'll get no chiggrel." But jeffer noned.

To make a long story short, the eeld'm soon met a briny and asked it to quench jeffer. But briny noned.

Then she found a broady and asked it to horn briny. But broady noned.

Then she found a broady kimmey and asked him to kill broady. But broady kimmey noned.

So eeld'm piked to a rope and asked it to hang kimmey. But rope noned.

Then eeld'm found a rat and asked it to chiggrel rope. But rat noned.

She piked on to a pusseek, and pusseek harped, "If you'll pike to yon broady and charl her for me, I'll chiggrel the rat."

So she piked to the broady. But broady harped, "If you'll pike to the haystack and fetch me some chiggrel, I'll charl myself for pusseek."

So eeld'm did what broady asked, and broady chiggreled and pusseek horned.

Then pusseek began to kill rat, rat began to chiggrel rope, rope began to hang broady kimmey, broady kimmey began to kill broady, broady began to horn briny, briny began to quench jeffer, jeffer began to ark stick, stick began to dreek hareem, hareem began to chiggrel borp, borp began to jump relf and pike region, and eeld'm got her chiggrel.

Words from Boontling

angry - cocked
bad - nonch
Boonville resident -
   Boonter
candy - dulcey
cat (female) - pusseek

coffee - zeese
cow - broady
dance - hob
deer - bosh
dog - hareem
to drink - to horn

to drive - to jape
to eat - to chiggrel
to eat too much - to gorm
to embarrass - to Charlie
rail fence - relf
fib, harmless lie - wes

fight - fister
fire - jeffer
food, meal - chiggrel
girl - applehead
to go, to travel - to pike
good - bal

greedy, a greedy person -
   heelch

haircut - hedge

half dollar - forbes

to hit, beat, whip - to dreek

home, one's home - region

to laugh - to hoot

man - kimmey

to milk a cow -
   to charl a broady

money - higs

to have lots of money -
   to be higged .

to have no money -
   to be dehigged

a nickel - a buckey

ocean - briny

old woman - eeld'm

pig, hog - borp

policeman - high-heeler

reading glasses - glimmers

to refuse - to none

rich - high pockety

rich person - high pockets

to save, to hoard -
   to chipmunk

schoolteacher - schoolch

to see, to notice - to deek

shoe - cloddy

dirty socks -
   pack-'em-out-billies

to speak - to harp

to step out - to branch out

storyteller - bearman

sunny days - sunnies

a tattler - a Jenny Beck

teenager - tweed

to telephone - to levi

temper tantrum -
   to have a greeny

woman - applehead

to wreck, break - to ark

young man - kimmey

young woman - applehead

For more bal stuff, branch out and pike on!

SOLUTIONS TO PRACTICE PROBLEMS

Pig Latin

1. Hide behind a bush and make a noise like a carrot.
2. A coyote. I put in the cement to make it harder.
3. You would turn red, too, if you had to change in front of all those people.
4. A failure.

Iggity

1. And found he was eating his shoe.
2. And slipped through the straw and fell in.
3. And nobody knows where she went.

Ku

1. . . . the siren said to the policeman.
2. . . . the cow said as she wandered down the road.
3. . . . the girl said, falling off a log.
4. . . . the doctor said as he looked at the patient's knee.

Obby-Dobby, Eggo-Peggo, Ip

1. "George, you are going down in history."
2. If it didn't, it would fall down.
3. Root beer.
4. You hold its nose.

Kinyume

1. . . . said Tom S. craftily.
2. . . . said Tom S. gleefully.
3. "Be careful with that knife . . ."
4. "What do seven days make?"

B Language

1. Teacher: "Now, let's look at the next word."
2. "A doughnut got fresh."
3. "The light was on. So he thought that somebody was home upstairs."
4. "Her mother made her take it back."

Sa-La

along came
the morning train—
peanut butter!

watching a tadpole
turn into—
a frog.

Medical Greek

The Story of the Vicious Bull

Two men suddenly were charged by a vicious bull. One of them climbed a tree. The other jumped into a deep hole, but he kept jumping out. When the bull charged at him, he jumped back in. Then suddenly he jumped back out, ran for the tree, and climbed it.

"Why aren't you in that hole?" his friend asked.

"Well," he said, "thar's a b'ar in that hole."

The Cat's Elbow

1. Three.
2. No cat has two tails. One cat has one tail more than no cat. Therefore, one cat has three tails.
3. The people who went fishing were a boy, his father, and his grandfather. The boy's grandfather also was his father's father.

Ziph

I laughed so hard I thought I'd die.
I did die.
They buried me,
and a little flower
   grew on my grave.
But the roots grew down and tickled me . . .

King Tut

a barn dance?   an ocean wave?   a moonbeam?
a peanut stand?   a barber shop?   a kitchen sink?

Thief Talk

A Poem in Thief Talk

As I sat in front of the fire
Warming me feet
There came a knock at the door
That made me old heart beat.

Boontling

The Old Woman and the Pig

An old woman found some half dollars and nickels and felt wealthy. So she went to Boonville and used her money for a pig.

On the way home, the old woman had to go over a rail fence. But pig wouldn't go, and she couldn't drive him home, and she wanted her dinner.

Soon a dog came by, and the old woman said, "Dog, dog, eat pig, pig won't jump fence and go home, and I'll get no dinner." But dog refused.

Old woman got angry and said to a stick, "Stick, stick,

beat dog, dog won't eat pig, pig won't jump fence and go home, and I'll get no dinner." But stick refused.

Soon she met a fire. Still in a tantrum, she said, "Fire, fire, break stick, stick won't beat dog, dog won't eat pig, pig won't jump fence and go home, and I'll get no dinner." But fire refused.

To make a long story short, the old woman soon met an ocean and asked it to quench fire. But ocean refused.

Then she found a cow and asked it to drink ocean. But cow refused.

Then she found a cow man and asked him to kill cow. But cow man refused.

So old woman went to a rope and asked it to hang cow man. But rope refused.

Then old woman found a rat and asked it to eat rope. But rat refused.

She went on to a cat, and cat said, "If you'll go to yon cow and milk her for me, I'll eat the rat."

So she went to the cow. But cow said, "If you'll go to the haystack and fetch me some food, I'll milk myself for cat."

So old woman did what cow asked, and cow ate and cat drank.

Then cat began to kill rat, rat began to eat rope, rope began to hang cow man, cow man began to kill cow, cow began to drink ocean, ocean began to quench fire, fire began to break stick, stick began to beat dog, dog began to eat pig, pig began to jump fence and go home, and old woman got her dinner.

NOTES
SOURCES
BIBLIOGRAPHY

Abbreviations in Notes, Sources, and Bibliography

AS *American Speech*

BL *Boys' Life*, "Think and Grin" columns

CFQ *California Folklore Quarterly*

JAF *Journal of American Folklore*

KFR *Kentucky Folklore Record*

MFA Maryland Folklore Archive, University of Maryland, College Park, Md.

NFA Northeast Archives of Folklore and Oral History, University of Maine, Orono, Me.

NYFA Folklore Archive, New York State Historical Association, Cooperstown, N.Y.

NYFL *New York Folklore, New York Folklore Quarterly*

RU Compiler's collection of folklore contributed by his students at Rutgers University, New Brunswick, N.J., 1963–78

SFQ *Southern Folklore Quarterly*

WF *Western Folklore*

NOTES

The publications cited are described in the Bibliography.

Am Ur-Quell. In the 1890s, readers of *Am Ur-Quell*, a German folklore journal, were asked to submit any secret language they knew. They sent in over 150 languages and variants which had been used in everyday life by children or adults in Europe, Africa, and Asia. It probably is the richest collection of secret languages ever published. A number of the languages in this book are from that material.

Secret Dialects. Only a few secret languages are distinct languages, with their own grammar, spelling rules, and pronunciation. Romany, the Gypsy tongue, probably is the best known of these.

Most secret languages are dialects or varieties of a speaker's native language, with only a few differences between one and the other. But these differences make a secret language almost incomprehensible to an outsider.

Converting an everyday language to a secret language involves one or more mechanisms. These are the ones most commonly used:

1. Moving a syllable from one position in a word to another position. (Pig Latin)
2. Transposing individual letters. (Medical Greek)
3. Adding a syllable or a letter. (Iggity, The Cat's Elbow)
4. Repeating a syllable. (B Language)
5. Substituting new letters or new words. (King Tut, Thief Talk)

Often, the same mechanism has come into use in several countries. Iggity, a New York State language, is one example. It depends on the same mechanism as *Nosa*, a Japanese language, and as *Sa*, a language used in the Bakoli tribe in Zaire. See Sherzer, p. 30.

Whistles and Drums. Secret languages are used only in speaking. Unlike codes and ciphers, they are not used in writing. But there are two secret languages which are not spoken in the traditional way. One involves whistling. It is used by the Mazataca Indians of Oaxaca, Mexico. The other involves sounding a drum. It is used by various African tribes. Both the whistled speech and the drumming reproduce the syllables, tones, and stresses one would use if a message actually were spoken. See Howell, pp. 192–97; Cowan, pp. 280–86.

Gree, Guy, Ire (p. 9). The suffixes used in Pig, Hog, and Dog Latin were used only in particular areas. "Gree" was reported from Glens Falls, N.Y.; "guy" from Cortland County, N.Y.; "ire" from Schenectady, N.Y.; "ly" and "ki" from Baltimore; "snikes" from an unidentified German city. They all were in use around the turn of the century. See Millard, p. 104; Hirshberg, pp. 27–28; *Am Ur-Quell* 3 (1892): 106.

Famous Sayings (p. 14). These perverted proverbs are called Wellerisms. They are named for Sam Weller, a character in *Pickwick Papers* by Charles Dickens. Mr. Weller used such sayings all the time. Wellerisms are distantly related to the proverb. Like the proverb, they provide a succinct observation drawn from experience and/or wisdom. Unlike the proverb, they conclude in a completely unexpected way.

Talking Backwards (p. 21). This kind of disguised speech is found in many countries. In England, petty thieves talk backwards, and so do some merchants and their helpers as they go about their business. What they say is called "Backslang." In Panama, Cuna Indians use this language, largely because they enjoy the word play. There it is called *Arepecumakke*, or "speaking backwards."

In France, it is called *le langage a l'envers* or "backwards language." Talking backwards is very popular with teenage gangs in Paris. But each gang has its own slang expressions. So an outsider must make two translations: from the disguised speech into the gang's argot, and from the argot into standard French. See Sherzer, p. 35; Opie, p. 320.

Champ Lop (p. 33). Transpositions like the ones in Medical Greek are sometimes regarded as Spoonerisms. But an actual

Spoonerism is created only when two real words result from the reversal of letters.

A good example of a Spoonerism is "a well-boiled icicle," which the speaker intended to be "a well-oiled bicycle." Another example is a "blushing crow," which started out, in the speaker's mind, as "a crushing blow." But "chamb lop"—that is, "lamb chop"—is just a transposition.

William A. Spooner is the person for whom the Spoonerism is named. He was a teacher and a minister at Oxford University from 1870 to 1930. His tendency to reverse letters delighted his students and others, who then deliberately created transpositions of their own. In fact, one scholar concluded that Spooner did not produce an unusual number of Spoonerisms, that most were contrived by others. But eventually all such reversals were given his name. See Robbins, pp. 457–62.

Thief Talk (p. 49). The secret language modern criminals use has been traced to the early fifteenth century to an argot used by roving bands of thieves, beggars, and tramps in Germany. Although this argot was based on German, it included many invented words and many terms from the Gypsy language Romany and from Hebrew, Turkish, and other languages. See Mencken, pp. 709–31.

Syllables and Sounds. Some linguists regard secret languages as an important source of data on various problems in linguistics. These include how speakers construct syllables and use them, how they represent various sounds, and the uses and importance they attribute to pronouns. See Sherzer, pp. 31–35.

SOURCES

The source of each item is given, along with variants and related information. Where available, the names of informants (I) are provided. Publications cited are described in the Bibliography.

page

i *Omtay's auntway. BL* 47 (7–57): 80.

5 *Pig Latin.* Oral tradition.

6 *What is the best way.* MFA, 1970.

What has fur. Clark, *SFQ* 25: 116. Variant: Cat. Ainsworth, *SFQ* 26: 268.

Why did the traffic light. RU, 1974.

What do you call. RU, 1974.

9 *Iggity.* I: Barbara Carmer Schwartz, Princeton, N.J., 1980. Childhood recollection from Delmar, N.Y., 1930s. Variant: Speaker inserts "iggity" after first sound in each word. Millard, *NYFL* 10: 104.

11 *There was an old man.* RU, 1972.

There was a young woman. BL 47 (6–60): 80.

There was an old lady. Compiler's recollection.

13 *Ku. Am Ur-Quell* 3: 167.

14 *"Don't touch me."* Esar, p. 82.

"I'm getting that rundown." MFA, 1974.

"This is really easy." Koch, *WF* 19: 196. Adapted slightly.

"Pretty swell joint." Esar, p. 80.

17 *Obby-Dobby.* NFA, I: Susan Scully, Orono, Me., 1976.

Eggo-Peggo. I: Sarah Ellis, Boston, Mass., 1979. Learned in Vancouver, B.C., about 1962. In United States also called Egg Latin; in England, called Eggy-Peggy. Opie, p. 320.

Ip. NFA, I: Susan Scully, Orono, Me., 1976.

18 *What did George Washington's father. BL* 68 (1–78): 80.

Why does a stork. Ainsworth, *SFQ* 26: 285.

What do cheerleaders. RU, 1974.

How do you keep a skunk. Essar, p. 23. Variant: A fish; cut off its nose. Schlesinger, *WF* 19: 192.

21 *Kinyume. Am Ur-Quell* 6: 37.

22 *"I wove this basket." BL* 53 (9–63): 86.

"I sing in the choir." BL 53 (9–63): 86.

"Eb fulcare." MFA, 1968.

"Thaw od ensev." MFA, 1968.

25 *B Language. Am Ur-Quell* 2: 22.

27 *Teacher: Sam, your spelling.* MFA, 1968.

Did you hear about the fight. NYFA, 1945.

Did you hear about the boy. Davidson, *SFQ* 7: 104. Adapted.

Did you hear about the girl. Esar, p. 111.

29 *Sa-La. Am Ur-Quell* 3: 188.

30 *A peanut sat.* Oral tradition.

A frog sat. Compiler's recollection.

33 *Medical Greek. Am Ur-Quell* 2: 79.

35 *The Story of the Bicious Vull.* Civil War era story as re-
counted in Randolph, p. 107. Adapted slightly.

37 *The Cat's Elbow. Am Ur-Quell* 2: 99.

38 *There was a goose.* Johnson, p. 150.

How can a cat. RU, 1974.

Two fathers and two sons. Ainsworth, *SFQ* 26: 291.

41 *Ziph. The Collected Writings of Thomas De Quincey,*
vol. 1, p. 202.

42 *The Flower.* Compiler learned this endless tale in Evans-
ton, Ill., about 1950. See Brunvand, pp. 117–18.

45 *King Tut.* Chrisman, *Science* 22: 305. Variants: *Am Ur-
Quell* 3: 135; Berkovits, *NYFL* 26: 148; Millard, *NYFL*
10: 105; Zim, pp. 110–11.

47 *Catfish.* Loomis, *WF* 9: 147.

Catwalk. Loomis, *WF* 9: 147.

Bubarurnun dudanuncute, others. I: Rachel Duronzio, 13;
Kenneth Duronzio, 12; Andrea Sherwin, 14; Alex Sherwin, 10; Princeton, N.J., 1979.

49 *Thief Talk.* Barnes, *JAF* 79; Maurer, *AS* 19; Troubridge,
AS 21; Wilde, *JAF* 2, 3.

50 *A Poem in Thief Talk.* Troubridge, *AS* 21: 46.

50 *Words from Thief Talk.* Barnes, *JAF* 79: 601–6; Maurer,
AS 19; 190–95; Mencken, pp. 709–31; Troubridge, *AS*
21: 45–47; Wilde, *JAF* 2: 304–5; Wilde, *JAF* 3: 305–10.

53 *Boontling.* Adams; Carranco, Simmons, *AS* 39; Rawles,
WF 25.

56 *The Eeld'm and the Borp.* Carranco, Simmons, *AS* 39: 284–86. Shortened and adapted slightly.

58 *Words from Boontling.* Adams; Carranco, Simmons, *AS* 39: 280–83; Chrétien, *CFQ* 1: 96; Rawles, *WF* 25: 98–102.

BIBLIOGRAPHY

Secret Languages

Adams, Charles C. *Boontling: An American Lingo.* Austin, Texas: University of Texas Press, 1971.

Am Ur-Quell. F. S. Kraus, ed. Vol. 2 (1891): 22–23, 48–49, 65, 79–80, 98–99, 111–12, 127–28, 143–44, 187–89; Vol. 3 (1892): 43–44, 106–7, 135–36, 167, 225–26, 328, 344; Vol. 4 (1893): 76–78; Vol. 5 (1894): 74–78; Vol. 6 (1896): 37–40.

Barnes, Daniel R. "An Early American Collection of Rogues' Cant." *JAF* 79 (1966): 600–7.

Berkovits, Rochele. "Secret Languages of Schoolchildren." *NYFL* 26 (1970): 127–52.

Burling, Robbins. *Man's Many Voices*. New York: Holt, Rine-hart and Winston, 1970.

Carranco, Lynwood and Wilma Rawles Simmons. "The Boon-ville Language of Northern California." *AS* 39 (1964): 278–86.

Chrétian, C. Douglas. "Boontling." *CFQ* 1 (1942): 96–97.

Chrisman, Oscar. "Secret Language." *Science* 22 (1893): 303–5.

The Collected Writings of Thomas De Quincey. David Masson, ed. New ed., vol. 1. Edinburgh, Scotland: Adam and Charles Black, 1889–1890.

Cowan, George C. "Mazteco Whistled Speech." *Language* 24 (1948): 280–86.

Farb, Peter. *Word Play: What Happens When People Talk*. New York: Alfred A. Knopf, 1974.

Greer, Dale. "Secret Speech." *KFR* 10 (1964): 35.

Hirshberg, Leonard K. "Dog Latin and Sparrow Languages Used by Baltimore Children." *Pedagogical Seminary* 20 (1913): 257–58.

Howell, Richard W. and Harold J. Vetter. *Language in Be-havior*. New York: Human Sciences Press, 1976.

Jespersen, Otto. *Language: Its Nature, Development and Origin*. New York: Henry Holt and Company, 1923.

Johnson, Clifton. *What They Say in New England and Other American Folklore*. Boston: Lee and Shepherd, 1896. Reprint edition: Carl A. Withers, ed. New York: Columbia University Press, 1963.

Maurer, D. W. " 'Australian' Rhyming Argot in the American Underworld." *AS* 19 (1944): 183–85.

Mencken, H. L. *The American Language: An Inquiry into the Development of English in the United States.* Abridged ed. Raven I. McDavid, Jr., ed. New York: Alfred A. Knopf, 1979.

Millard, Eugenia L. "What Does It Mean?—The Lore of Secret Languages." *NYFL* 10 (1954): 103–10.

Newell, William Wells. *Games and Songs of American Children.* New York: Harper and Brothers, 1883. Reprint edition: New York, Dover Publications, 1963.

Opie, Iona and Peter. *The Lore and Language of Schoolchildren.* London: Oxford University Press, 1959.

Partridge, Eric. *A Dictionary of Slang and Unconventional English.* 5th ed. New York: The Macmillan Company, 1961.

Rawles, Myrtle Read. " 'Boontling'—Esoteric Speech of Boonville, California." *WF* 25 (1966): 93–103.

Sherzer, Joel. "Play Languages: Implications for (Socio) Linguistics." *Speech Play: Research and Resources for Studying Linguistic Creativity*, pp. 19–36. Barbara Kirshenblatt-Gimblett, ed. Philadelphia: University of Pennsylvania Press, 1976.

Troubridge, St. Vincent. "Some Notes on Rhyming Argot." *AS* 21 (1946): 45–47.

"U.S. Public High School." *Life* 35 (12–14–53): 153. An article on Tut language as it was used in Davenport, Iowa.

Wilde, W. C. "Some Notes on Thief Talk." *JAF* 3 (1890): 303–10.

———. "Some Words on Thief Talk." *JAF* 2 (1889): 301–6.

Other Folklore Genres

Ainsworth, Catherine H. "Black and White and Said All Over." *SFQ* 26 (1962): 263–95.

Brunvand, Jan H. *The Study of American Folklore: An Introduction*. 2nd ed. New York: W. W. Norton & Company, 1978.

Clark, Joseph D. "Riddles from North Carolina." *SFQ* 25 (1961): 113–25.

Davidson, Levette J. "Moron Stories." *SFQ* 7 (1943): 101–4.

Esar, Evan. *The Humor of Humor*. New York: Horizon Press, 1952.

Johnson, Clifton. *What They Say in New England and Other Folklore*. See "Secret Languages," above.

Koch, William E. "More Wellerisms from Kansas." *WF* 19 (1960): 196.

Loomis, C. Grant. "Traditional American Wordplay." *WF* 9 (1950): 147–52.

Randolph, Vance. *We Always Lie to Strangers: Tall Tales from the Ozarks*. New York: Columbia University Press, 1951.

Robbins, Russell H. "The Warden's Wordplay: Toward a Redefinition of the Spoonerism." *Dalhousie Review* 46 (1966–67): 457–65.

Schlesinger, Marilyn R. "Riddling Questions from Los Angeles High School Students." *WF* 19 (1960) 191–95.

Withers, Carl A. *A Rocket in My Pocket: The Rhymes and Chants of Young Americans*. New York: Henry Holt and Company, 1948.

Zim, Herbert S. *Codes and Secret Writing*. New York: William Morrow & Company, 1948.